An Artist Goes Bananas

Paul McDonald

Indigo Dreams Publishing

First Edition: Paul McDonald
First published in Great Britain in 2012 by:
Indigo Dreams Publishing
132 Hinckley Road
Stoney Stanton
Leicestershire
LE9 4LN

www.indigodreams.co.uk

ISBN 978-1-907401-68-8

British Library Cataloguing in Publication Data. A CIP record for this book can be obtained from the British Library.

Designed and typeset in Palatino Linotype by Indigo Dreams.
Cover design by Ronnie Goodyer at IDP

Printed and bound in Great Britain by The Russell Press Ltd. www.russellpress.com on FSC paper and board sourced from sustainable forests.

I don't think I'll bother with a dedication.

Acknowledgements

Acknowledgements are due to the editors of the following journals in which some of these poems first appeared. *Apparatus; The Arcadian; Burning Houses; The Delinquent; Flash: The International Short-Short Story Magazine; The Little Episodes Anthology; Neon Literary Magazine; Orbis; The Smoking Poet; Social-i; Streetcake Magazine; Soul Feathers Anthology.*

'Author Observed at the Hay-on-Wye Festival' appeared in the pamphlet, *A Funny Old Game* (Norfolk: Michael Green). The found poem, 'Emily Jane Felton' is a slightly rearranged version of a Facebook status update, and I thank Emily Jane Mole (née Felton) for permission to reproduce it.

Other Publications by Paul McDonald

Poetry
The Right Suggestion (1999)
Catch a Falling Tortoise (2007)

Novels
Surviving Sting (2001)
Kiss Me Softly, Amy Turtle (2004)
Do I Love You? (2008)

Criticism
Fiction from the Furnace (2002)
Students Guide to Philip Roth (2003)
Laughing at the Darkness (2011)

As Editor
Loffing Matters (2006)

CONTENTS

An Artist Goes Bananas

New York Poet

I see you at the Amory Square Hospital, Ward K,
or third in line for soup,
a war humming in the distance.
I see you eye-to-eye with Peter, smiling beneath

your beard at his clean shaven chin.
Or with Bill, posing below a fake seashore,
your elbow at his crotch, his hand on your venerable neck.
Sometimes you're too theatrical

in Byronic shirt and workman's trousers;
sometimes like Christ in a nightdress;
or tough, the hardest chorister in the choir.
I prefer you listening to a child's whisper.

You're at your best in Brooklyn,
your hand beneath your waistcoat
checking heart, force, fibre.
You think your eyes are dull, but they're dazzling.

An Hour, Maybe Two

It's coming,
hurting things along the way.
It throttled Mrs Lanford's self-esteem,
and left her lodger, Nigel, with tortured thoughts.
Mr Kumar's dreams suddenly turned sour
and he closed his shop.
Rumour is he's torched it but I'm too afraid to look.
My next door neighbour, Sharon, killed her cat;
my own stays out of reach.

They warned us, but who'd have guessed at this?
Now the Helpline is no longer manned; the radio's white noise.
I wait, though waiting hurts.

Bad Seed

She blew a parting in my hair
like a dandelion clock
and told me I was going bald.
That was the week before she chucked me.

She went from strength to strength
and wed the year the harvest made the news.

Yesterday I spotted her in Tescos,
twenty years older, cherry-picking fruit.
I watched her pick it up, just to put it down;
I watched her tap a melon
like a doctor taps a chest, and frown.

Charlie's Art

Charlie in elephant trunk trousers
swapping his left eye for a light bulb.

Charlie filming a cat's shadow.
Charlie drinking ink, crying shapes onto a blotter.

Charlie with a see-through skull and mashed potato brain,
the Mona Lisa's smile where his sulk should be.

Charlie has a surfboard tongue!
Pastoral Chas is green in a suit made of chlorophyll.
Is that Charlie in a burka?

Charlie paints an image in the mirror.
Charlie calls it: *Charlie Calling it Charlie.*

Real Men

At eighteen the best jobs
are the ones you can do hung-over.
Cutting leather was a bad one.
The ruthless knives sliced bone.
I sobered up smartish,
but my mate Mick would say:
Real men don't need fingertips.
At thirty six he knew the ropes,
made finger-slings from pigskin:
You wax the seams,
he said, *to stop the blood*
from seeping through.
I think about him often.
He'd cadge my fags
and snap the filters off,
ask me if I thought I was a girl.

Him

I've seen him in the starch of a potato,
I've seen him on a pancake.
I've seen him on a tree trunk eyeing dogs,
and in a jar of Marmite.

Ultrasound revealed him once
hiding in a womb.
I've seen him on a ceiling tile looking like a poet,
and in a swirl of ice-cream.

He was symmetrical on moth wings;
a reflection in a Stratocaster's shine.
He's been in peaches, puddles, planks of wood,
twice in a dune.

Mostly he's in clouds
but he's also been a road stain and a slice of toast.
This morning he was present in my grimy sink,
waiting to be cleansed.

Better Than A Bloke

My gran would fart for fun and,
when bladdered, liked to show her bloomers.
They were special ones saved for going out,
billowing with lace and frills.

Age seven at the Liberal Club in Walsall
I'd watch her through a Vimto bottle lens.
She'd lift her skirt up like a woman in the
company of mice, high kick to the Can Can,

and holler to the room:
I'm booting Bernie in the balls!
Bernie was my granddad. Mom and dad would
cringe behind Babycham and shandy,

but can laugh about it now. The time she
broke a blind woman's glasses, or choked
when a bottle top lodged in her throat.
Regulars would say she was better than a bloke.

On The Wilmslow Road

Litter on the wet pavement
indigestion at the bus stop
man in orange jacket
with his head in a hole.

Yellow barrier supplied by Enterprise Plc.
Wet leaves on the pavement
yellow lines on the road
and red lines on the road.

Rooms to Rent in Rusholme!

A yellow generator
a yellow wire leading to temporary traffic lights
on amber. Sandbags keep a sign in place:
Temporary Traffic Lights.

A Lambert & Butler cigarette box,
a Ribena bottle and Red Bull tin.
A wood pigeon on the pavement (alive).

Someone has abolished roaming charges this summer.
Half a wheel trim and a blue plastic bag on the pavement.
A question: Well Driven?

A yellow hard hat; a blue hard hat.

Arrows at war: Beware Oncoming Traffic.
Bouquets around a lamppost
wet petals on the curry mile.

Magic Mirror

Her magic mirror vanished.
Her mind was somewhere else
when it disappeared:
she blinked to find a space where
her image should have been.
It made much of her achievements.
It was her proof that she is here
and she'd see herself transformed in it,
optimism framed in it.
She could submerge in it and breathe,
locate herself in light.
It was gravity: without it she might float away.
She wishes she could glimpse it now
and see herself reclaimed by it:
her doppelganger back behind her eyes.

Author Observed At The Hay-on-Wye Festival

Hay is the border 'Town of Books' where
in a late spring week the authors come.
One I watch wears a seersucker suit
and sports a straw hat. He looks as if he should
be smoking cheroots in a bohemian cafe.
The black mountains brood over his comings
and goings: his demure 'thank you's and his

jiffy bag of scripts, underlined and asterisked.
In a marquee stuffed with smiles he solicits
applause, easy in the eager attic full of bats.
He gives his complimentary rose gallantly to a
girl, and signs fifty flyleaves beneath a hundred
eyes. He asks if Hay is England, or if it counts
as Wales, as he dines out free on anecdotes in

the Swan Hotel. On the streets he strides like you
and I, though augmented by his fame; we watch him
tip the buskers, absorbing silent stares. He
takes attention with him within Hay's bookshop
walls where he wanders like a tourist, perusing
patient spines. Engrossed he moves from shelf to
dusty book lined shelf, scrutinising volumes, looking for himself.

Little Left To Do

We tried to bring the thing to life
by basting it with juices, and baking.
We buried it with nitrates and watered.
We tied it to a kite and waited for a lightning storm.
We coaxed a cow to lick it, a guinea fowl to sit on it.
We searched the Net for pills, ground them in a mortar,
and sprinkled spice of powder blue. We bullied it.
You good-copped and I bad-copped: it stood its ground.
Incantations didn't work, nor prayer.
I raved, you cried, but nothing changed.
There is little left to do but leave it, I suppose. But we can't.

Tips For Conversing With Them

The best ones can open wine bottles
with a nod of the head.
Light obeys them, so prepare to be impressed.

They move with poise like snowfall,
hover hairsbreadths over ground,
a metre if they're showing off.

Their hearts are shaped like hearts in art -
the kind seen in Christ's chest - or so it's said.
Don't mention wings: they envy angels

and long to cast inspiring shadows, like Gabriel.
Ask questions: What colour's heaven?
How large is small? Is that perfume

I can smell, or is it you?
They'll respond in snorts and sighs,
but sometimes carve replies

in the air before you:
Are you surprised we are so beautiful?
Be sure to answer yes.

The Road I'd Like To Be

I'd like to be a road -
a winding one that takes
you where you need to go.
A road lined with hedges
short enough so you
can see the sights you pass:
Rape seed fields, pylons, Little Chefs.
There'll be signposts citing miles
to go before your journey's end.

My surface will be strong and hard:
tyres, feet, and horses' hooves caress
the kind of road I'd be.
Not a Roman road:
they're too predictable.
I want to be a curvy one with Z bends.
I want to be the kind that says:
Ride me to your perfect place,
with luck you'll live to see it.

Story Spinner

No one wants to write about
your whispered secrets
or read the scribble that makes

strangeness stranger.
You wore a madman's coat,
muttered,

smoke obscuring half closed lids.
But I recall you
spiral-eyed,

spinning tales:
the girl who built cathedrals out of kitten fur,
the man who ate a gypsy's lips

for fun.
Everything depended on them:
imparted charms.

I recall them all,
your characters like flames,
risky to ignore.

Sugar Beetle

My doctor informs me that I'm suffering from sugar beetle. I think he enjoys telling me because he punctuates his pronouncement with kisses to his knuckles: right fist, then left. My symptoms are classic, apparently: the overnight appearance of a burnt sugar exoskeleton, and a tendency to be smug about the longevity and diversity of my kind. The cure is beyond my capacity to pay, so the prognosis is disheartening. I have become a delicacy for humans (the bastards), and my life is in danger. I will be consumed, his says, with relish. By relish he means enjoyment, not condiment. He gives me a month, less if I don't wear a burka.

Your Reflection

It angers your reflection if you wear a pencil moustache drawn with a pen. Please use a real pencil. Don't try to catch it out that way. Don't wink at it either - reflections loathe irony. Remember when you steamed that glass, wrote 'mist' in the mist, and thought it clever? Your reflection hated that. Don't try to make it laugh. You know you can't do jokes and so does your reflection. Cook it something nice instead: chilli sometimes makes it smile, although that might be wind. And DO NOT kiss it! When you close your eyes it won't. Imagine that.

Off The Rails

You give me bad advice which I fail to take. I follow the falling sun, and you follow me. I walk, trot, run, jump on a bus to a quiet part of town. I see my face in a window. You're at my shoulder, smiling. I hear bridges crack, cars in the distance crash. Flights are aborted, trams abandon their rails. Everything is shrinking.

Trying Not To

I have toads for sale, he says, knocking at the door.
They have elastic legs and clear bright eyes.
He knocks again. We crouch in silence
on the other side, flinching with each fist beat.
They sweat the sweetest wine, he says,

and smile all the time. I've twenty in a box.
Then his knocks aren't knocks at all, but kicks.
I'll kill them one by one unless they're bought.
Still we crouch, quiet, trying not to tremble.
Could we bear their tiny squeals?

It's Snowing
(after Ana Blandiana)

It's snowing with happiness,
the snow falls with glee
above waters giddy with joy,
above trees ecstatic with mirth
above rapturous birds.
It snows as if the fish
feel new born.
It snows
with the power of people –
deliciously it's snowing.
No one is shocked.
Only I know
that snowfall was misery.
It's early
and beautifully it's snowing,
and my mind starts working
and for once
it's useful and
for once the wolf is happy to starve.

Noel Road

From the curb we ponder 25,
strain to see inside the space that framed them:
the shrinking walls hung with splintered smiles.

It's easy to imagine.
Sex, satire – too weird even for the 60s;
sardines and custard in the afternoons,

evenings spent corrupting Mrs Sayers.
Neighbours flinched at every parrot shriek
as laughter cracked plaster and loosened slates.

We like the thought of them, despite the spume
of blood that geysers now and then
in the current tenant's nightmares.

We take a photograph for reasons they would
chuckle at: it's been long enough to laugh again.
We pretend to hear them snigger as we walk away.

Cradled

He'd confront a hurricane for her.
He wouldn't waver in it:
he'd swell to meet it like a sail.
He is immense and getting bigger,

observable from distance now,
like something on the landscape
you would photograph, or sketch.
If she'd anticipated this

she might have reconsidered,
but he shields her when she's vulnerable,
cradles her far above the earth
where the highest flying birds

struggle to make nests.
Now she can sense him
when her eyes are closed:
his shadow, the groan of his expanding.

Spring Cleaning

Open the window,
let that bee in before it kills itself
against the glass.
The buzz will do us good.

Let the air flow –
a breeze of pollen and green scent.
Let the spirit of the cat back
to claw carpet pile,

rub her face against the sideboard.
The room is cooler with her here.
And free whatever needs escape:
the reek of winter, the budgie's cheek,

the jazz that longs to
irritate our neighbour as he trims his hedge.
The words I wrote in March will be wiser
when they've had a chance to breathe.

Hotter Than Expected

The sky is blacker
than the pigeons' eyes,
blacker than they've seen it.
They know the storm is
due and so do we.

Hoardings sell us nothing now,
no travel, petrol, plastic;
no one chooses Vodaphone or Virgin,
or contemplates the card without a fee.
The young blame the old

but we're all regretting something.
Silent flashes frame
our blistered frowns
as someone lists things
that could have saved us –

mirrors in the desert,
re-established grasslands, etc.
Suddenly there's thunder in our heads
and the raindrops,
hotter than expected, are red.

L.A. Poet

Cast from the prom
for being Satan,
you caught a pen

that fell from heaven,
charted missions:
to save wild dogs,

to be one, to walk
the railway tracks alone.
You fought for fun,

fell from stools, for women:
Tina, Georgina, Cupcakes.
You decked the world

with walnut scowls, but survive:
a rumour in the Frolic Room,
cooled by shadows.

Dave In The District

Girls in silver shorts and cowboy hats;
girls in corsets pointing pierced tongues at Dave.
He only window shops but they
tap the glass at him with square, painted nails.
Some talk at mobile phones: *I'm sitting in a window*;

others contemplate the dark canal,
a neon heart's reflection.
Dave doesn't want to like it here:
trouble clots at corners with hyena types
sniffing for a tourist with a limp.

Strip club doormen give him stick
just for passing by; they can't coax him to a show.
Dave lacks that kind of dough
so presses on, drawn against his will
to window after window, feeling nude.

Jezebel

Remember when we rolled one
in a page of *The Sun*
sealed with Green Shield Stamps?

It made the cat go peculiar,
the curtains smell like Amsterdam.
We watched the midnight movie,

served Bette Davis cider
through the television screen,
and laughed over

words that rhyme with *Jezebel*.
You were as crazy as I've seen you,
begging me to choke you with my tongue.

We feasted on each others lips,
closed our eyes and waited while
the clock went back in time.

Did you ever stop floating?
I did, in the end, but every time
I think of you I levitate.

Over Here

Where have you been?
I've been over there.
You've been over there?
Yes, I've been over there.
Have you come over here, now?
No.
Then why are you here?
I'm here to tell you I'm there.
So you're staying?
Yes.

The Thing

It plays havoc in the house,
smothering light, chilling rooms,
making her Chihuahua yap at empty space.

She can't trust in its existence,
like someone else's dream,
but its company shrinks flesh.

When it visits her at night
exhalations fog the air
as if she breathes it into being.

It taps her pillow for attention
and she gives it, getting nothing in exchange
but excruciating clarity, and fear.

Tramlines

Dave at the station
listening:
wires crackle,
energy slips shackles.

Dave among the travellers' eyes
on the tram
with headlines,
twitching lips, tapping feet,
a tannoy calling stations.

Dave counting time,
guessing speed
and distance.

Dave reading signs:
No cycles, smoking, feet on seats,
food, drink, or spitting.
Do not distract the driver.

Dave needing something his reflection sees.

Dave slipping shackles,
chasing.

System Drained

He is wearing a damp parker,
tracksuit bottoms and trainers.
The neighbours would shun him
but the ducks he used to feed
come running from the pond.

At the windows he is shocked
by rooms devoid of stuff:
a baffled lounge, a kitchen straining
for an echo. A sign across the taps says:
SYSTEM DRAINED.

There's nothing in his pocket where
a key should be, though there's a spare
beneath the decking in the garden.
It reminds him of the knock that
wouldn't stop; the drilled lock.

Webs

I watch a watermark appear -
filament by filament –
a pattern of the kind
forever waiting to emerge
like a fingerprint.

Such schemes
are hatched in seeds,
smiles, spider's webs.
They're in myths
that structure dreams,
as well as wobbling air,
skewering life
with rightness.

Behind the eyes
something always lurks,
radiates and lures.
Like a magnet.

Applause

In the streets that front
the sun beyond the iron gates
life's crowds hurry.
He can see them
as he sits in silent thunder,
sucking current from the air.

Above the sky is
indigo and dubious.
He puts his forehead
to the window and feels
decision in his nose.
A flash of silver follows,
then applause.

Crooked Smiles

I'm not a mirror,
but you search for yourself in me.
You shouldn't: I'm a fraud.
But of course that's why you love me.

My worlds keep you hooked,
like titbits that I drip-feed in my storyteller style.
I'm a master of the poignant plot,
plus I have nice teeth.
Unless I need to make you laugh,
then crooked smiles are funny.

Here's a good one:
my words are what you think with,
my eyes are what you see with,
and every time you talk you're a liar.

Emily Jayne Felton (found poem)

Ceremony venue (booked)
Reception venue (booked)
Beckie's dress
Beckie's shoes
Bridesmaids' accessories (hairbands, necklaces)
My underwear □
Champagne glasses
My dress (ordered)
My accessories (tiara, necklace, earrings, fascinator)
Stuart's and my shoes

Daddy

The kid next door has tiny dots for eyes like the black bits at the centre of a pigeon's. I hate him. He is rough with his puppy and reckless with his balls. He plants things in the garden and glares when they fail to grow. He admires his mother's whistle. He's seven, and thinks he sees the point of things. He reminds me of the 80s, and senses that I'm poor. His screams pierce the wall - *daddy, daddy, daddy* – and he knows I can hear.

You Need Us

Need a no strings loan? New hope for addicts. Find that special someone or your money back. RE: Your compensation. Find singles in your street. Guaranteed jackpot every day. Important news from Jesus. Lara's on the lookout for lonely men. Injured? Take this compensation test. Psychic diagnoses. DIY Botox kits for less. Lara won't ask twice. Clear your debts, or money back. Cash and expenses paid for donors. Degree by correspondence: become an orthodontist. Viagra, Viagra. Too hairy? Ditch that gorilla vest: try Waxaway for less. Make jewellery from your teeth. Lara is still waiting. We know you know you need us.

Playa At Dawn

Spectating from the safety of my balcony, I watch them wade through blue-grey like men in metal boots or puppets with a string cut. They give each other donkey rides, take leaks against the palm trees, or climb them. One makes it halfway up, shouts something about coconuts, comes down empty-handed. Another spots me watching in my dressing gown, bawls: *Buenos Dias, Pedro!* in a Geordie accent. I feel their world tilting. When I wave, some wave back, but others give the finger. The Geordie bares his arse.

Almost Time

The wasps are dangerous and low,
dissatisfied with grass blades.
It's nearly time to die.
The sun can't clear the roof
or warm the apple tree
whose fruit lies brown and bursting
in the shade. I listen to it rot
as seedpods wilt on branches
and crows consume each other's curses.
The neighbour's cat displays
its vertebrae, yawns before departing:
he, or something like him, will be back.

Strange Bird

You could kiss a poem better,
charm it into life with fairy dust
shaken from your beard.

Wordsmith in a whirl
who paid his rent in art,
you painted dogs with hosepipe tails,

floating nudes,
glasses, bellies, broken teeth.
We long for what you were:

an elephant in Wellingtons;
walking, talking tambourine;
poetry machine.

Fishy

Tinned tuna's fine
but I don't like tuna steak.
It tastes too much like tuna.

I'm much the same with salmon
when it isn't smoked.
Don't talk to me of caviar

or sushi. I've never
liked the sound of them.
I hear they're far too fishy.

Brandy Lake

We stopped beside a lake
the day it turned to ice,
house brick thick and firm enough
to build a future on.

Sunshine froze before
it touched the earth
and tree roots drew a blank.
But sap was rising somewhere
and we became a counter to the frost
as throat-sounds rubbed together
and together struck
a fire to set the lake ablaze:
a brandy lit to warm the lips of winter.

For Sale

Here upon the eastern shore
a host of vessels huddle
and traders crying melodies
are hugging crates.
Each summer fancy rises
over articles for sale:
melons with their hearts on fire,
pinks in pots and
(dog-eyed in the afternoon)
people.

The Soul Of Spring

One dull day in March
he pulls his woollen hat
below his ears.
All he sees is desert:
too little for a poem of one word.
No snappy clothes, no drink.
No cards, dice, or horses.
No sporting girls.
All he has is hunger
like a tramp, or a holy man.

One fine day in May
he throws his woollen hat
onto a hook.
The soul of spring thrills
him into season,
stiffens him to sugar.
Now is when it all begins,
the list of kicks:
the man who juggles knives
in an overcoat of fur;
the acrobat who swings
between two chairs. Or better.
The play performed to ringing bells;
the banjoist; the peasants
stroking gipsy folk on fiddles.

BTW, FYI

Sorry to leave yet
another note on the fridge.
It's not about plums.
I wanted you to know I'm
annoyed about last night.
You and your performance!
It reminded me painfully
of every other instance.
Don't think I'll let it drop
that easily this time.
You could make reparation,
I suppose, by dropping by the
pharmacy to pick up my prescription.
BTW, FYI
Your kitten has confessed.

Rhymes

George Gershwin's great isn't he?
And Ira too I guess.
I can't quote any songs for
fear of copyright, but they're ace.
The ones that Fred Astaire sang;
the theme tune from *Manhatten*, etc.
They turn my head to fizzy pop,
build stairways up to paradise.
Sometimes I search for hours
for words that rhyme with Gershwin.
It's hard. George is easier in this respect.
And Ira too I guess.

Don't Ask, Just Do

From one to the other they kick it –
side-foot, toe-poke, back-heel.
It rolls without screaming, or knowing why,
and we watch not knowing what.

A puffer fish; crew cut cat.
The shape of hat
a tasteless head would wear.
The sphere on which all spheres are based.

A monkey brain.
The kernel of the seed from which
the tree of knowledge grew.
Marble moon. *The* moon.

My mother's helmet.
Ghandi's rupture, if he had one,
my dad's if he didn't.
A famous fruit (not that one).

Rubber bands banding bands.
A brontosaurus heart in my sister's bathing cap.
The devil's thought-balloon in a Biblical cartoon.
It must be kept in motion: all things are true.

Three Recipes And A Cure

1
Take the life you could have led
and make a story of it. Don't write it down:
sing it to a mirror in a voice that isn't yours.
THINK: would your reflection like the other you?

2
On your birthday –
the second of the minute of the hour that you were born –
drink your bathwater.

3
Find the church in which your mother was baptised.
Strip to your underclothes and lie upon the alter.
Ignore the vicar's plea to "respect this house of worship."
Don't move until the press have seen your prostrate form.

4
Go to sleep thinking of your fingerprint.
You'll dream of mazes –
turn left from the centre and you'll wind yourself free.

The Creative Use Of Teeth

You tell me of your ideal film –
the one you'd like to see (perhaps produce yourself).
It stars a woman, not unlike the one who's beaming
at me now, who finds a hundred thousand teeth.
She finds them in her Wellingtons,
she finds them in her purse, pockets, bra.
She steps into the shower and is ankle deep in teeth,
tips up her teapot and pours a cup of teeth.

The movie lasts a month.
Week one: the heroine finds teeth.
Week two: the heroine counts teeth.
Week three: she sleeps and dreams of teeth.
Week four: she makes a fortune crafting things from teeth -
bangles, broaches, necklaces –
then wins the love of one she loves:
a man with striking teeth.

I'll Give You 5

I'll check in to your hotel at 10pm. Like any normal person you'll be in the bar, so it's likely you won't see me. In my suitcase I'll have nothing but a badger, a hacksaw, and the *Book of Common Prayer*. I'll request the room above you. If that's not free I'll take the one next door or, at a pinch, below. At 10.45 I'll order coffee, take my pills. 3 will keep me up till 6. You'll return about 11, eat a complimentary mint then brush your teeth. At 12 you'll settle-down to sleep. I'll give you 5, and then begin.

I Ching

She'd say things like: "Why do people fuss about Karadzic's 'crimes against humanity' while Ronan Keating's still a free man?" And she claimed I made *her* laugh consulting the *I Ching* about consulting the *I Ching*. I fancied her, but where did I stand? On the day she left she grabbed me in the office, breathed on my specs and drew a tick in each lens. I'd been right, but what about?

September 30th, 11.59 pm

It's something that began when we moved in together. On the first day of every month, the first one to remember would pinch and punch the other, saying: 'A pinch and a punch, it's the first day of the month.' Sometimes she'd strike first, sometimes I was quicker. It soon became competitive and we'd contrive to wake up early, to beat each other to it. We'd set elaborate traps: I'd spring out of the wardrobe as she reached in for a blouse; she'd secrete herself beneath the bed, assault my slippered feet. Twenty years on, we're still the same. As each new month approaches we grow edgy: who will beat the other to the draw? But our edginess has undermined the fun.

I'm waiting for her now behind the curtains, like Polonius.

An Artist Goes Bananas

It began with muttering in his sleep,
then incoherent shouts once or twice a night.
Next hobbies: his mimes

seemed like semaphore, his photographs
of puddles were monochrome amoebae
with human nuclei.

He wrote a book on bees: their waggle dances.
He started saving hair, finding stories
in the pattern of his dinner plate. Then circling:

turning on himself like a dog about to settle.
Yesterday he claimed his life is art
in a speech lasting longer

than it should have.
Today, written in the misted mirror,
a message: *Tomorrow I will peel myself.*

Indigo Dreams Publishing
132, Hinckley Road
Stoney Stanton
Leicestershire
LE9 4LN
www.indigodreams.co.uk

Papers used by Indigo Dreams are recyclable products made from wood grown in
sustainable forests following the guidance of the Forest Stewardship Council.